Sing a song

Sing, sing, sing a song,
Sing a song together;

Sing, sing, sing a song,
Sing a song together.

Come, come, come to tea,
Come to tea together;

Come, come, come to tea,
Come to tea together.

In, in, in the bath,
In the bath together;

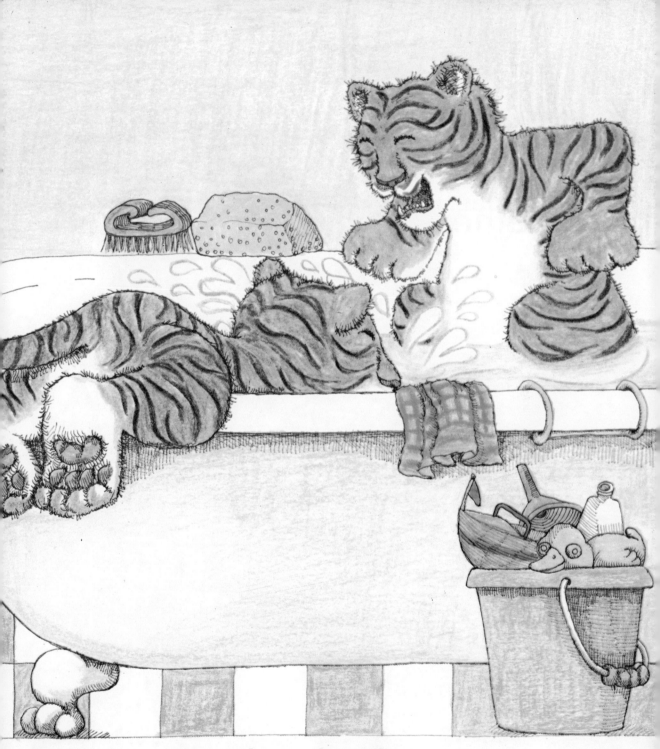

In, in, in the bath,
In the bath together.

Splash, splash,
splash about,
Splash about
together;

Splash, splash, splash about, Splash about together.

Out, out, out we jump,
Out we jump together;

Out, out, out we jump,
Out we jump together.

Off, off, off to bed,
Off to bed together;

Off, off, off to bed,
Off to bed together.

Read, read, read a book,
Read a book together;
Read, read, read a book,
Read a book together.

Tuck, tuck, tuck us in,
Tuck us in together;
Tuck, tuck, tuck us in,
Tuck us in together.

Fast, fast, fast asleep,
Fast asleep together;
Fast, fast, fast asleep,
Fast asleep together.